I0410901

Opportunities and Challenges for the Export of U.S. Value-added Wood Products to China

Scott Bowe

Matt Bumgardner

Terry Mace

United States Department
of Agriculture

Forest Service

Northern Research Station
General Technical Report
NRS-35

ABSTRACT

This report explores some of the opportunities for, and challenges associated with, exporting wood products to China. Five topics are examined: an overview of trends in forestry and forest products in China, export opportunities and challenges for U.S. primary wood producers (Study 1), export opportunities and challenges for U.S. secondary wood producers (Study 2), relevant barriers to trade, and a compilation of state export resources. This work is based on observations from three trade missions to China (March 2004, March 2005, and July 2006), interviews with persons knowledgeable with hardwood markets in China, and two surveys of Chinese forest products business groups.

ABOUT THE AUTHORS

- SCOTT BOWE is an Associate Professor and Wood Products Specialist at the University of Wisconsin Madison.
- MATT BUMGARDNER is a Forest Products Technologist with the U.S. Forest Service, Northern Research Station, Princeton, West Virginia.
- TERRY MACE is a Utilization and Marketing Specialist, Division of Forestry, Wisconsin Department of Natural Resources, Madison, Wisconsin.

ACKNOWLEDGMENTS

- The work upon which this publication is based was funded in whole or in part through a grant awarded by the Wood Education and Resource Center, Northeastern Area State and Private Forestry, Forest Service, U.S. Department of Agriculture.
- Technical support was provided by Hongmei Gu, owner of B One Technology Consulting Company in Madison, Wisconsin.
- The authors would also like to thank Paul Swenson for his invaluable assistance with our three trade missions to China and subsequent data collection. Paul Swenson is Director, Council of Great Lakes Governors, Shared China Trade Office, Shanghai, China • www.TheChinaHand.com

CHINA'S FOREST RESOURCE AND WOOD RAW MATERIALS

Forests covered 174.9 million hectares in China in 2003, according to the State Forestry Administration, accounting for 18.2 percent of the country's land area. This represents a gain of more than 52 million hectares since the mid 1970s when forest cover was 12.7 percent. Further, China's forest stocking volume totaled 12.5 billion m³ in 2003 (Jiang 2007). Since the implementation of economic reforms in 1978, China's economy has grown at an unprecedented rate. As a result, China imports large volumes of wood raw material to satisfy its growing demand as domestic production falls far short of demand. Total industrial consumption of roundwood was 310 million m³ in 2004, but national timber production was only 52 million m³ (Jiang 2007).

In 2004, China imported 7.3 million m³ of tropical logs, making it the world's largest importer of such logs. Malaysia, Papua New Guinea, Gabon, Myanmar, and the Republic of Congo were the primary sources. Further, China also imported 19 million m³ of temperate logs with Russia providing the bulk of this volume. China also is the world's largest importer of tropical sawn wood, accounting for almost 3 million m³ or 27 percent of all tropical sawn wood imports worldwide in 2004 (International Tropical Timber Organization 2006b). By contrast, approximately 1.2 million m³ of temperate hardwood lumber was imported by China in 2004 (Petry and Qing 2007).

A recent study of Chinese import trends since the 1990s showed that forest products are increasingly entering the country in less processed states as more value is being added to the products by Chinese manufacturers. Examples ranged from increased log imports to boost domestic plywood production to increased pulp imports to support more paper production, all at the expense of finished plywood and paper imports (White et al. 2006). Logs and lumber are China's most rapidly growing primary import segments (Table 1) (Zhu 2006).

Table 1.—China import volumes (1,000 m³) of primary wood products, 2000 and 2004 (Zhu 2006)

Product	2000	2004	Percent change
Softwood logs	6,397	15,962	149.5
Hardwood logs	7,215	10,282	42.6
Sawn hardwood	3,168	4,304	35.9
Sawn softwood	468	1,700	263.2
Plywood	1,003	780	-22.2
Veneer	650	223	-65.7

Specialty burl veneer being produced by a Chinese manufacturer from imported logs. Photo used with permission of Terry Mace, Division of Forestry, Wisconsin Department of Natural Resources.

CHINA'S WOOD PRODUCTS PRODUCTION AND TRADE

China's wood products manufacturing industry is large, diverse, and growing rapidly. China realized a trade surplus in forest products for the first time in 2005, when exports rose by 29 percent from 2004 to $20 billion; imports increased by just 8 percent to $18 billion (International Tropical Timber Organization 2006a). In 2006, the value of China's forest industry output was $146 billion[1], a 26 percent increase from 2005. Of this total, the value of the primary industry came to $64.5 billion, up eight percent from 2005. The value of the secondary forestry industry was $71.2 billion, exceeding the primary forestry industry for the first time, a 49 percent increase from 2005 (Global Wood 2007). Other examples of growth include the output of wood based panels, such as plywood, fiberboard, and particleboard, which increased 8 percent, 20 percent, and 46 percent, respectively, from 2005 to 2006 (Global Wood 2007). The output of China's wood flooring industry was 292 million m[2] in 2005, up 18 percent from 2004. Of this total, solid composite flooring accounted for 46 million m[2] (40 percent increase), laminated flooring was 190 million m[2] (20 percent increase), bamboo flooring was 6 million m[2] (20 percent increase), and solid flooring was 50 million m[2] (30 percent decrease) (Global Wood 2006). Wood consumption by industrial application is shown in Table 2; construction and paper production consumes the largest quantities (Zhu 2006).

China's wood products industry remains a diverse mixture of establishments, ranging in size from very large production lines to small scale enterprises to handicraft shops; smaller facilities represent the majority of firms in the industry (Petry and Qing 2007). Many of the largest furniture companies provide dormitory style housing for their employees in areas where housing is not readily available.

Table 2.—Chinese wood consumption by application and quantity (1,000 m^3), 2004 (Zhu 2006)

Application	Quantity	Percent of total
Paper	96,800	32.8
Construction	63,500	21.5
Agriculture	40,000	13.6
Furniture	26,500	9.0
Export	18,900	6.4
Pit/mine prop	11,000	3.7
Other	38,300	13.0

A small hardwood flooring operation in China. Photo used with permission of Scott Bowe, University of Wisconsin-Madison.

Hand-carved banisters produced at a very small Chinese workshop. Photo used with permission of Terry Mace, Division of Forestry, Wisconsin Department of Natural Resources.

[1]All currency values in this report are reported in United States dollars unless specified otherwise.

China has become the largest furniture producer and exporter in the world (Petry and Qing 2007). Annual gross output of furniture increased from $9.5 billion in 1997 to $25 billion in 2003, an average annual increase of 17 percent; exported furniture shipments increased a staggering 560 percent during the same period, reaching $7.3 billion in 2003 (Cao et al. 2004). More recent reports put the value of China's furniture exports at $13.8 billion in 2005, with about one third being wood furniture (Butterworth and Lei 2006). Even though China is the world's largest exporter of furniture, more than 70 percent of the gross output of furniture in China was consumed by the domestic Chinese market in 2002 (Cao et al. 2004), and this trend has continued to the present (Petry and Qing 2007).

China's main solid wood products exports by value are furniture and panel products, mostly plywood (Table 3) (Wagner 2007). Relying largely on China's low labor and operational costs (Cao et al. 2004), there is a focus on production and export of more labor intensive and processed products. In the first quarter of 2007, exports of wooden furniture grew to 60.4 million pieces ($2.2 billion in value), a 36.7 percent increase from the same period in 2006. Nearly half ($1.1 billion) of these furniture exports went to the United States, with about $0.2 billion each going to Hong Kong SAR, the United Kingdom, Japan, and Canada (International Tropical Timber Organization 2007).

Table 3.—China export value (million dollars) of solid wood products by type, 2006 (Wagner 2007)

Product	Value	Percent of total
Furniture	3,427	53.3
Plywood/fiberboard	1,126	17.5
Construction related (joinery, carpentry, flooring, marquetry)	819	12.7
Lumber/rough wood	137	2.1
Other wood products	920	14.3

Dormitory housing at a large Chinese furniture factory. Photo used with permission of Terry Mace, Division of Forestry, Wisconsin Department of Natural Resources.

Furniture on display in the showroom of a Chinese manufacturing plant. This style of furniture is quite ornate with detailed carvings and is well made. This group was targeted for the European market. Photo used with permission of Scott Bowe, University of Wisconsin-Madison.

CHINA'S POTENTIAL DOMESTIC MARKET FOR WOOD PRODUCTS

In addition to China's rapidly expanding wood export sector, the domestic market for wood products also is growing. Rapid economic growth and the deregulation of the housing sector in China have expanded the interior decoration and furnishings market. Development and construction projects are common scenes in China's large and medium sized cities. The intense domestic competition in the furniture and decoration business in recent years and the dramatic changes in consumption patterns have pushed up the demand for wood products. Rapid economic growth and remarkable housing expansion have created a new generation of increasingly affluent, savvy consumers who are eager to outfit their living space with quality interior decoration and furnishings, potentially made with U.S. hardwoods. For example, it is estimated that China's middle class (families with assets of $18,072 to $36,144) comprises about 20 percent of the population. This translates into about 250 million people, a number equal to about 85 percent of the population of the entire United States.

Predictions place the Chinese middle class at 40 percent of their population by 2020 (Hardwood Review 2007).

Housing data for China can be inconsistent. Some sources show there were 24 million new housing starts in 2005, based upon an average residence size of 80 m² (Braden 2006). As a comparison of relative market size, the United States had about 2.1 million housing starts in 2005 (U.S. Census Bureau n.d.a), with an average size of 226 m² for single family units and 116 m² for multifamily units (U.S. Census Bureau n.d.b). Other sources suggest 10 to 12 million housing starts annually in China (Boardman 2006) or 16 to 18 million starts (Butterworth and Lei 2006). Despite the data inconsistencies, the major point is that the scope and scale of the housing market in China is enormous.

In addition, the Chinese government is focusing on the development of rural areas. There are 700 million peasants living in rural China; the standard of living in rural areas is very low by western standards and represents a large and undeveloped market. It is predicted that there will be rapid development in rural areas of China in the coming years a huge potential market for wood products.

Tower cranes at numerous construction sites like these fill the skylines in China's major cities, creating potential markets for wood furnishings and fixtures. Photo used with permission of Terry Mace, Division of Forestry, Wisconsin Department of Natural Resources.

INTRODUCTION

In recent years, United States domestic production of secondary wood products has declined due to the shift to offshore production facilities, such as those found in China (Schuler and Buehlmann 2003). As production has moved offshore, these producers have sourced hardwood lumber from countries across the globe. Domestic lumber producers need to participate in these markets to remain competitive in the global marketplace. Exports account for approximately 10 percent of all hardwood lumber produced in the United States (Hardwood Market Report 2005) and China is an important destination. According to data from the U.S. Census Bureau[3], China (including Hong Kong) accounted for approximately 19 percent by volume and 15 percent by value of United States hardwood lumber exports in 2004. The major species breakdown of this volume is as follows: red alder (*Alnus rubra*), 22 percent; yellow poplar (*Liriodendron tulipifera*), 19 percent; oaks (*Quercus* spp.), 17 percent; and maples (*Acer* spp.), 9 percent.

Domestic hardwood lumber producers need a better understanding of how these foreign markets operate. For example, U.S. suppliers learned early on that Chinese buyers purchase lumber mostly on price and not on grade (Barford 2004). In other words, U.S. suppliers have to determine the proper mix of grades to include in a shipment to meet the specified price.

The United States is generally a high cost source in a global context, which potentially puts its producers at a comparative disadvantage (Butterworth and Lei 2005) and also puts pressure on profit margins. For example, the average nominal price of United States hardwood lumber exported to Asia has declined in recent years as China, following a low production cost model, has become the major market in the region. In contrast, average nominal price to Europe has increased (Bumgardner and Hansen 2001).

There is limited market channel and product information available on hardwood lumber markets in China. In this study, we have taken initial steps to profile hardwood lumber market channels in China, providing much needed information for companies that seek to be competitive in the global marketplace. Understanding this information will give U.S. hardwood lumber exporters an advantage in the Chinese market. The primary objectives were to identify the primary market channels through which hardwood lumber flows into the Chinese manufacturing sector and to determine the hardwood lumber specifications imported by Chinese wood manufacturing firms.

A wood market in southern China. Photo used with permission of Scott Bowe, University of Wisconsin-Madison.

---

[2] This section is based in part on a study conducted in 2005 by authors of this publication (Bowe et al. 2007).

[3] Assessed from lumber export database (available from the authors) maintained by the U.S. Forest Service, Princeton, WV.

STUDY DESCRIPTION

Data were collected utilizing a written questionnaire and short interviews using intercept procedures and on site interviews. The questionnaire development and data collection procedures are described below.

The questionnaire was developed with the assistance of persons familiar with the hardwood lumber export industry, including personnel from the University of Wisconsin, the U.S. Forest Service, the Wisconsin Department of Natural Resources, and the Council of Great Lakes Governors in Shanghai, China. The questions were designed to collect information on import channels within the Chinese wood manufacturing industry. Questions covered the following topics related to hardwood lumber purchases: volume, grade, species, country of origin, and types of sales agent used. The questionnaire fit on one page, front and back, and was designed to facilitate efficiency of data collection and respondent cooperation.

A native Chinese speaking wood scientist at the University of Minnesota translated the English questionnaire into Mandarin Chinese. The translated questionnaire was pretested in China with Chinese business representatives familiar with the hardwood lumber industry. Minor translation changes were made to improve understanding.

Data were collected during short personal interviews with hardwood lumber using firms. The primary data collection points during the trade mission (March 2005) occurred during three industry trade shows: the China Famous Furniture Trade Show in Dongguan, the International Construction & Decorative Material Exhibition in Dalian, and the China 2005 WoodMac FurniTeck WoodBuild International Exhibition in Shanghai. During the shows, the trade delegation maintained exhibition space representing the Lake States Lumber Association; most of the data collection occurred from these exhibition spaces.

In addition, four interviews were completed during company tours in the cities of Dongguan and Dalian. These tours were organized with the assistance of the Dongguan Furniture Association and the Dalian Furniture Association.

Native Chinese speakers from the staff of the Council of Great Lakes Governors and the University of Minnesota conducted the interviews and recorded the information on the survey form. Interviews typically lasted five minutes or less. Company presidents or production managers were targeted for the interviews. During the trade shows, these individuals were identified by their trade show name badges and through business card exchanges.

Responding Firms

Forty five companies participated in the survey. Two questionnaires were incomplete resulting in 43 usable responses.

The types of companies sampled used hardwood lumber in some component of their business. Furniture manufacturers represented 30 percent (n=13) of the respondents, followed by lumber brokers at 26 percent (n=11), flooring companies at 12 percent (n=5), and wood markets at 12 percent (n=5). Wood markets in China can best be described as a shopping mall for wood. Individual wholesalers lease garage like space and sell raw materials to local wood manufacturers. Lumber, veneer, panel products, and other wood materials are available, with much of the stock imported.

Twenty one percent (n=9) of the respondents indicated other business types. These businesses included veneer, cabinet, window, and door manufacturers. In addition, three of the furniture manufacturers indicated that they also brokered hardwood lumber as a part of their business.

STUDY 1: OPPORTUNITIES AND CHALLENGES FOR PRIMARY PRODUCERS

Geographic Distribution of Responding Firms

China consists of 23 provinces, five autonomous regions, four municipalities, and two special administrative regions (Fig. 1). Study participants had facilities located in eight provinces, one municipality, and one special administrative region (Table 4). The largest numbers of responses were from Shanghai and Guangdong, likely due to the primary data collection point at the trade shows in those regions and the large concentration of wood manufacturers in the Guangdong province.

Responding Firms' Representative

Respondents representing the participating firms included sales managers (37 percent, n=16), company presidents (30 percent, n=13), lumber buyers (12 percent, n=5), and production managers (9 percent, n=4). Other company representatives (12 percent, n=5) included positions such as general managers, inspectors, and engineering personnel. Several respondents held multiple positions within their company. These types of respondents would be knowledgeable of their company's overall hardwood lumber purchases and use.

Table 4.—Location of responding firms

Location	Number of facilities	Location	Number of facilities	Location	Number of facilities
Shanghai	17	Guangdong	13	Liaoning	4
Zhejiang	3	Hong Kong	3	Hebei	2
Jiangsu	2	Jilin	2	Shandong	2
		Taiwan	1		

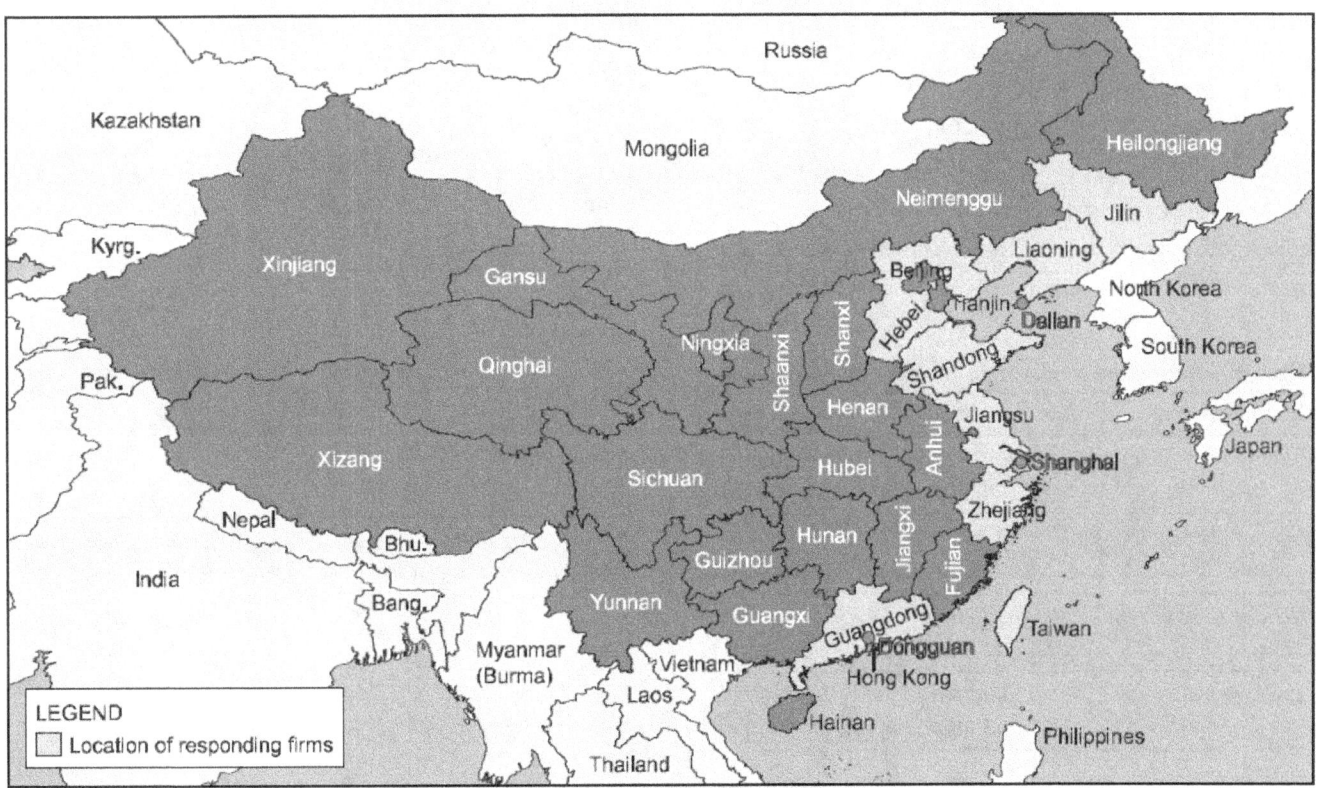

Figure 1.—China map with respondent locations shaded and major ports indicated.

LESSONS LEARNED

Hardwood Lumber Consumption and Sources

Annual hardwood lumber consumption in 2004 for all responding firms was 1.5 million m^3 (665 million board feet). Median hardwood lumber volume used by respondent firms was 5,380 m^3 (2.4 million board feet), and the mean was 38,700 m^3 (17.4 million board feet). Table 5 shows lumber use by company type; the means and medians for each company type are similar with the exception of furniture, where two very large firms skewed the mean (with these two firms removed, the mean was 5,851 m^3 and the median was 3,000 m^3).

Respondents were asked what proportion of their hardwood lumber came from the United States. The median imported volume was 33.0 percent, while the mean imported volume was 38.7 percent. Other sources suggest that China imports approximately 10 to 20 percent of its hardwood lumber from the United States (Barford 2004, American Hardwood Export Council 2005). Imports of U.S. hardwood lumber ranged from zero to 100 percent with 32 percent (n=12) of the responding firms purchasing no lumber from the United States and 18 percent (n=7) purchasing 90 percent or more of their hardwood lumber from the United States.

Table 5.—Hardwood lumber use by company type, 2004

Company type	Mean	Median
Furniture manufacturers (n 10)	124,700 m^3 (56,120,000 bd ft)	4,000 m^3 (1,800,000 bd ft)
Lumber brokers (n 11)	7,364 m^3 (3,314,000 bd ft)	5,760 m^3 (2,592,000 bd ft)
Wood markets (n 4)	5,375 m^3 (2,419,000 bd ft)	5,750 m^3 (2,588,000 bd ft)
Other (n 13)	9,429 m^3 (4,243,000 bd ft)	6,480 m^3 (2,916,000 bd ft)

When asked to rank the top three countries supplying their hardwood lumber, the United States was ranked number one by 18 of the responding companies and fell into the top three rankings 24 times (Table 6). A scoring system was used where a first ranking = 3 points, second ranking = 2 points, and third ranking = 1 point. Under this system, the United States scored nearly three times higher than the next country, Russia. Russia, Africa[4], and Germany also ranked within the top three at least six times and showed correspondingly high scores (Table 6).

Table 6.— Top hardwood lumber sources by country/region

Country/region	First source[a]	Second source	Third source	Score[b]
United States	18	1	5	61
Russia	6	2	-	22
Brazil	3	2	-	13
Germany	1	4	1	12
Indonesia	2	2	1	11
Africa	1	2	3	10
Canada	1	3	1	10
Southeast Asia	2	1	1	9
Europe	1	2	-	7
New Zealand	1	1	2	7
Malaysia	-	3	1	7
Thailand	1	1	1	6
Burma	1	-	1	4
China	1	-	-	3
Romania	1	-	-	3
South America	-	1	1	3
Austria	-	1	-	2
Chile	-	1	-	2
France	-	1	-	2
Gabon	-	-	2	2
Ukraine	-	1	-	2
Korea	-	-	1	1

[a] For first, second and third choice, n=40, n=29 and n=21, respectively.
[b] Based on first=3 points, second=2 points, third=1 point.

---

[4] Some respondents reported specific countries while others reported general regions.

Hardwood Lumber Import Channels

The hardwood lumber import channels used by the Chinese manufacturers are described in Table 7. The top three channels were mainland Chinese brokers, Chinese wood markets, and direct from United States manufacturers, which captured 60 percent of the responses when combined. Chinese brokers and Chinese wood markets serve as channel intermediaries between the raw material country of origin and the Chinese wood manufacturers.

Thirty six of the respondents reported the percentages of their hardwood lumber purchases that moved through the various import channels. As shown in Table 7, 39 percent (n=13) of the respondents purchase exclusively through one channel, the remaining 61 percent (n=22) purchase their hardwood lumber through two or more channels.

Primary ports of entry were numerous. The respondents identified more than 15 port cities. Shanghai and Hong Kong were cited most frequently, representing a combined 42 percent of the responses. The primary ports of entry into China are Hong Kong, Shanghai, and Dalian (Fig. 1).

Table 7.—Hardwood lumber import channels for Chinese manufacturers

Channel	Frequency	Frequency of exclusive purchases
Mainland Chinese broker	16	2
Chinese wood market	15	2
Direct from U.S. manufacturer	15	3
U.S. broker	8	2
Taiwanese broker	8	1
Japanese broker	1	-
Other	14	3

Examples of U.S. hardwood lumber exported to a wood market in China. Photo used with permission of Terry Mace, Division of Forestry, Wisconsin Department of Natural Resources.

Hardwood Lumber Grades Imported from the United States

The hardwood lumber grades imported from the United States are described in Table 8. The top two grades were Firsts and Seconds (FAS) and #1 Common, representing the highest frequency by the respondents. This is contrary to other reports, which cite the Chinese preference for lower grade (and price) hardwood lumber (Barford 2004). Regarding special grades, several respondents identified dimension parts as a "grade" that they were interested in buying. For example, dimension of 20 mm x 108 mm x 910 mm (0.79 in x 4.25 in x 35.8 in) would be used as flooring blanks and be machined into a solid hardwood flooring product.

The hardwood lumber grading rules developed and implemented by the National Hardwood Lumber Association (NHLA), though voluntary, are complex (National Hardwood Lumber Association 2003). Questions were included within the survey to ascertain the level of understanding of the NHLA grade rules.

We collected data about the respondents' understanding of minimum width, minimum length, and allowable defects of grade FAS boards. According to the NHLA rules, the minimum width is 15.2 cm (6.0 in) and the minimum length is 2.4 m (8.0 ft). Only one respondent closely identified the minimum width, stating 15 cm (5.9 in) with the median response being much smaller at 10 cm (3.9 in) (Table 9). Only one respondent correctly identified the minimum length of 2.4 m (8.0 ft). The remaining respondents were closer on the length with several listing values close to 2.4 m (8.0 ft). The median for the minimum length responses was 2.0 m (6.6 ft), lower than the actual rule.

Regarding allowable defects within the FAS grade, a simple categorical scale of "none," "very few," "some," and "many" was included. The first three categories, "none," "very few," and "some" were selected one, nine, and eight times, respectively. The relatively high occurrence of the "some" category may indicate that the respondents believed that more defects were allowable in the FAS grade than were actually the case. None of the 18 respondents providing data for this question selected the "many" category.

Given this apparent lack of understanding of NHLA grading rules, we were interested in learning if the respondents believed that they had received subgrade lumber from the United States. Eighteen of 24 respondents answering this question indicated that they had received shipments of subgrade lumber. When asked what percentage of the shipment was downgraded, the median response was 10 percent and answers ranged from three percent to 20 percent. Due to the inherent variability in hardwood lumber and judgment of the lumber grader, NHLA grading rules allow for 5 percent variation in the value of the shipment before the unit is considered misgraded.

On several occasions, anecdotal evidence from wood market tours during the trade missions suggested possible confusion regarding United States lumber grades. In one example, we found clear defect free hardwood boards, which were too narrow and too short to qualify for the FAS grade; however, the sales agent insisted that the lumber was FAS.

Table 8.—Hardwood lumber grades imported from the United States

NHLA grade	Frequency	Frequency of exclusive purchases
FAS	14	3
Select	5	2
#1 Common	14	1
#2 Common	9	-
#3 Common	1	-
Special grades	1	-

Table 9.—Respondents' knowledge of NHLA FAS grade rules

Dimension	FAS rule	Respondents (median)	Respondents (range)
Minimum width	15.2 cm (6.0 in)	10.0 cm (3.9 in)	2.5 cm to 35.5 cm (1.0 in to 14.0 in)
Minimum length	2.4 m (8.0 ft)	2.0 m (6.6 ft)	0.3 m to 4.0 m (1.0 ft to 13.1 ft)

Major Hardwood Lumber Species

Respondents were asked to indicate the top three species of hardwood lumber imported and the country or region of origin for each of these species. The results are described in Table 10. Oak was the most frequently cited species, including red and white oak from the United States as well as "Chinese" oak from eastern and northern Asia. Maple also was cited frequently, as was a collection of tropical and softwood species. Walnut (*Juglans* spp.) also was an important species. A number of lesser cited species included birch (*Betula* spp.), ash (*Fraxinus* spp.), beech (*Fagus* spp.), alder, yellow poplar, and cherry (*Prunus* spp.). It should be noted, however, that U.S. Census Bureau data indicate that alder and yellow poplar are the two most abundant species exported from the United States to China. A lone mention of basswood (*Tilia* spp.) from Russia was made by a producer of Venetian blinds.

The United States position was particularly strong for oak and walnut; it also was strong for ash, alder, yellow poplar, and cherry, though these species were mentioned less frequently. This is not surprising given that some of these species, particularly yellow poplar, do not occur commercially on a large scale outside of North America. Interestingly, it seems there is a fair amount of international competition associated with maple, even though most commercial maple production occurs in North America. This could indicate that channels more complex than "direct from the United States" are being employed and the ultimate source of maple lumber is being masked. It also could indicate that "trade names" sometimes confuse efforts to identify species botanically (Fig. 2).

Table 10.—Summary of the major species of hardwood lumber used by respondents and country or region of origin for each of the species[a]

Species	Number of times cited	Country/region of origin[b]
Oak	30	United States (23); Russia (4); Germany (3); China (2); Europe (1)
Maple	16	United States (10); China (2); Germany (2); Europe (1); Russia (1); Korea (1); Indonesia (1)
Tropical species[c]	15	Brazil (6); Southeast Asia (3); Africa (2); Indonesia (2); Thailand (2); China (1); Burma (1)
Softwoods[d]	11	Russia (3); New Zealand (2); Canada (2); United States (2); Austria (1); Chile (1)
Walnut	10	United States (8); Europe (1)
Birch	4	China (3); Russia (1); Germany (1); Korea (1)
Ash	4	United States (3); China (1)
Beech	4	Germany (2); Romania (1); China (1)
Alder	3	United States (3)
Yellow-poplar	3	United States (3)
Cherry	3	United States (2); Canada (1)
Basswood	1	Russia (1)

[a] Respondents were asked to indicate the top three species of lumber used; results presented are aggregated.
[b] For a given species, this may not sum to "Number of times cited" because on occasion respondents left country of origin blank, and some listed multiple countries of origin for some species.
[c] Includes the following species: "teak" (n=3), rubberwood (*Hevea brasiliensis*) (n=2), lapacho (*Tabebuia* spp.) (n=2), and n=1 each for okoume (*Aucoumea* spp.), jatoba (*Hymenaea courbaril*), kempas (*Koompassia malaccensis*), ailanthus (*Ailanthus altissima*), sandalwood (*Santalum album*), "African species," "tropical species," and "hardwood species."
[d] Includes the following species: "pine" (*Pinus* spp.) (n=6), Douglas fir/hemlock (*Pseudotsuga menziesii* Mirb./*Tsuga canadensis*) (n=2), and n=1 each for radiata pine (*Pinus radiata*), southern pine (*Pinus* spp.), and tamarack (*Larix laricina*).

The United States does not seem to be competitive in terms of birch exports, as sources in eastern and northern Asia were most common. Additionally, most beech exports came from Europe. Collectively, tropical species seem to represent a formidable threat to United States species, with Brazil and Southeast Asia leading as sources in this category (note that in addition to "Southeast Asia" specific Asian countries, such as Indonesia and Thailand, also are mentioned). Also notable was the collective presence of softwoods, with North America sharing the spotlight with Russia and the largely plantation based sources of New Zealand and Chile.

A "wall" of Russian birch lumber at a Chinese wood market. Note that this lumber was unloaded and stacked by hand. Photo used with permission of Scott Bowe, University of Wisconsin-Madison.

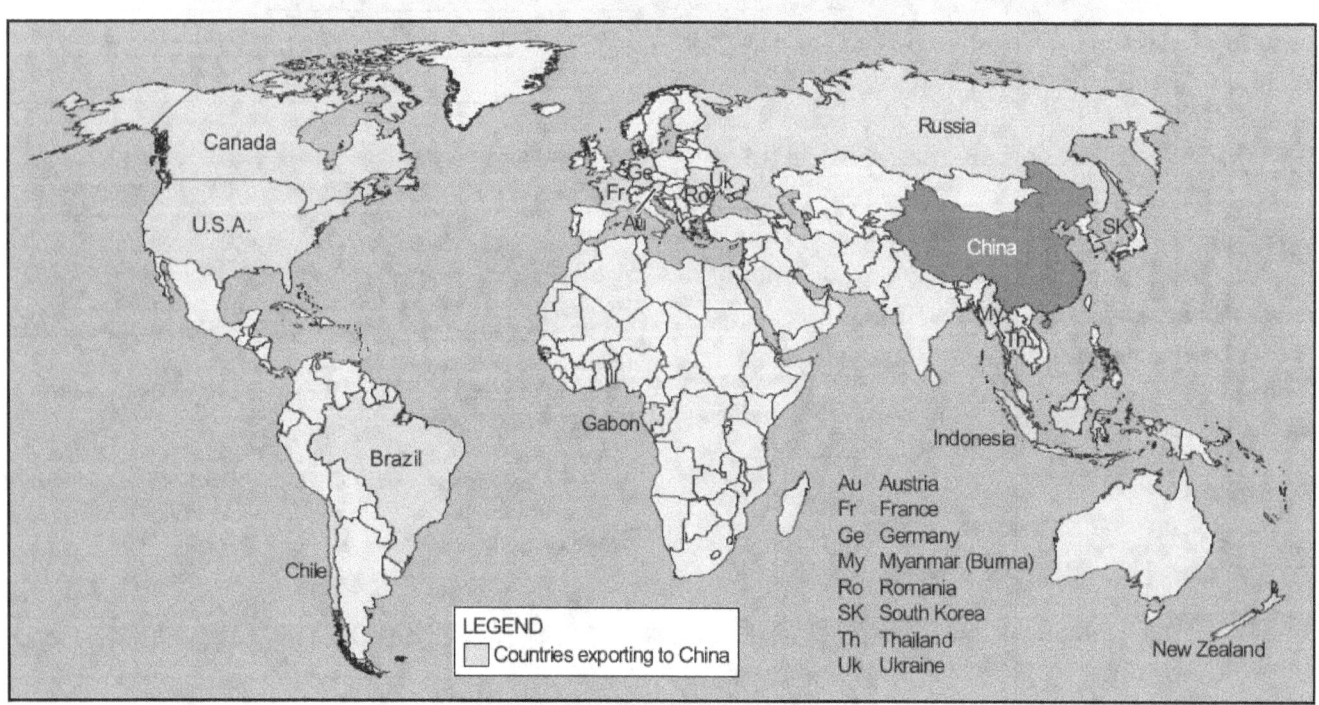

Figure 2.—World map with countries cited as hardwood lumber sources for China shaded.

PRIMARY PRODUCER CASE EXAMPLES

Case 1: Lumber Exports to China

A hardwood lumber producer based in the U.S. Lake States region aggressively approached the Chinese market for a 5 year period starting in 2002. This firm has several large sawmills and significant kiln capacity producing kiln dried northern hardwoods. To be successful in the Chinese lumber market, a company must invest a significant amount of time and money to develop potential contacts and foster business relationships. Some U.S. firms have chosen not to develop a physical presence in China but rather sell to brokers or wholesalers. Others have tried to develop an on the ground presence in China and have chosen to hire an agent to represent their products and interests. An agent may represent only one firm or several companies at the same time. In this case, the firm hired a sales agent representing only their company. Managers from headquarters traveled to China on a regular basis to meet with the agent and sales prospects. This brought the face of the company to China and added validity during sales meetings. Interestingly, the firm had initially hired an agent that represented more that one company. After several years of limited success, they terminated the multiple agent and hired an agent as a sole representative.

Trade shows have been useful tools in bringing buyers and the company's representatives together. In fact, China is now home to the largest collection of wood industry trade shows in the world, surpassing European trade shows in size and attendance. In this case, the firm found participating in trade shows in Beijing, Guangzhou, and Dalian to be an especially efficient way to find customers.

Regarding their product mix, this company has had success exporting hardwood logs and kiln dried hardwood lumber to China. Conventional wisdom suggests that the freight disadvantage from the Lake States region compared to more coastal states would place northern hardwoods at a disadvantage. However, this firm has overcome the freight disadvantage with a species advantage.

Walnut, which has limited commercial growing range within the United States, makes up a large portion of their exports in logs and lumber. White oak and red oak comprises much of their remaining lumber exports. They have the capability to source southern oak species to accommodate pricing and margin issues. Although the endeavor was not profitable for the first years, the company is now turning a profit in this market. Exporting lumber and logs to China required commitment, patience, and a significant investment in time and money.

Case 2: Lumber Exports to China

Another company located in the upper Midwest began an investigation into the hardwood lumber export market in China. The company produced green and kiln dried hardwood lumber. The firm hired a Chinese national living in the United States to assist their staff in identifying markets in China. The Chinese employee had a degree in forest products from a Chinese university and had numerous contacts within the Chinese forest products industry. The management staff and Chinese employee made several trips to China looking for high end furniture manufacturers who desired a higher grade of lumber. They were targeting this segment with the hope that it would be less sensitive to the added inland freight costs and higher cost of northern hardwoods as compared to southern or Appalachian hardwoods.

After about 6 months the effort was evaluated and they ended their efforts in China. The company decided that this market was not a good fit for their company even though their Chinese employee felt that they where very close to making sales to some of the high end furniture companies that were willing to pay more for the higher quality northern hardwoods.

13

CONCLUSIONS

Primary Products

Even though the data used in this report are preliminary due to small sample size, several tentative conclusions can be made. First, the United States faces numerous global competitors in the Chinese hardwood lumber market. Countries such as Russia and Brazil, as well as several from Southeast Asia, were not only cited as sources for hardwood lumber but also were found to be suppliers of some of the more common species exported to China. These imports included a number of tropical species, which can be used as substitutes for temperate species, as well as direct competitors to United States temperate species such as birch, oak, and beech. However, it has been noted that China is expected to increase imports of temperate hardwoods due to concerns over the price and future availability of tropical hardwoods; the United States is the leading source of temperate hardwoods to China (Butterworth and Lei 2005).

Second, there are many different channels being used to move hardwood lumber into China. Direct from United States manufacturers was found to be a major channel type, but there were many other channels of similar importance. The use of brokers and development of contacts within the Chinese wood market also are important and suggest that exporting to China can involve substantial investment in marketing research and development of selling arrangements.

Third, there seems to be considerable confusion among Chinese buyers over standard United States hardwood lumber grades. These buyers appear to be operating more under a pricing model, not a standard grade model. It could be that Chinese buyers and United States sellers are trading under a system with different understanding of the terminology and with United States sellers doing what is necessary to remain profitable at pricing levels demanded by Chinese customers.

More lumber product available at a local wood market in China. Photo used with permission of Scott Bowe, University of Wisconsin-Madison.

STUDY 2: OPPORTUNITIES AND CHALLENGES
FOR SECONDARY PRODUCERS

INTRODUCTION

It is often said of China: The high end markets are there, the challenge is to find them! This sentiment seems supported by demographic data. At the broadest level, there are 1.3 billion consumers in China. Middle class income in China is considered to be about $600 per month and upper class income is around $15,000 per year. Further, there are approximately 100 million people in the upper income categories.[5] This seems consistent with published reports that there are about 25 to 30 million middle class households in China with another 8 million affluent homes (University of Pennsylvania 2006a). About 400 million Chinese live in urban areas (University of Pennsylvania 2006a); conversely, there are 700 million peasants and China remains a country of extremes in purchasing power. We focus here on opportunities for export of value added hardwood products to middle and high end market in China.

A Chinese-made oak staircase in a high-end townhouse near Shanghai. Photo used with permission of Terry Mace, Division of Forestry, Wisconsin Department of Natural Resources.

A portion of the skyline of Shanghai, considered by many to be the modern financial center of China. Photo used with permission of Terry Mace, Division of Forestry, Wisconsin Department of Natural Resources.

---

[5] Based on information gathered from interviews conducted during the trade missions.

STUDY DESCRIPTION

How do hardwood companies find information on this potential market? One approach is to work with relevant trade associations. The Modern ArchiTectural Information Company (MATi), formed around 2001, is an association of designers and architects providing engineering support to design and architectural firms and their suppliers in China. MATi services include assistance with development of new products and specifications, as well as promotion of new products to designers and builders. Several MATi executives were interviewed on the trade mission and a survey of the membership was discussed. We later surveyed the membership of MATi (in the winter of 2007) to ascertain opportunities for export of value added hardwood products from the United States to China. Questions were designed to understand more about the product and service attributes desired by high end developers and architects in China. The questions were developed based on observations from the several trade missions to China.

Responding Firms

We received 102 usable responses. Eighty three percent of responding firms were architect or design firms so consequently 90 percent of respondents were architects or designers. Eighty six percent of the firms worked with interior finishing in their developments and 85 percent described themselves as operating at medium high to high price points. More than 97 percent of the firms operated in the Shanghai market; 14 percent operated in Beijing and 13 percent operated in other cities. While Shanghai and Beijing are the top investment destinations for real estate in China (Cao et al. 2006) numerous other "second tier" and smaller cities also are experiencing rapid growth. Shanghai is generally viewed as a more progressive market in terms of architecture and design while Beijing is generally thought of as more conservative.

Table 11 shows that the responding firms were developing a variety of property types as well, ranging from offices to single family housing. Approximately 80 percent of Chinese residents living in urban areas reside in multifamily high rise buildings, ranging from six floor walkups to luxury condominiums and apartments; only about 10 percent live in single family homes (Cao et al. 2006).

Table 11.—The types and percentages of real estate designed and/or developed by responding companies

Real estate type	Percent of firms involved
Office space	90.2
Multiple family housing (apartments)	77.5
Single-family housing (villa or townhouse)	70.6
Commercial space	70.6
Other	25.5

High-end townhouses outside of Shanghai, modeled after western developments. The superstructures are made of poured concrete and reinforcing bar. Such developments offer export opportunities for value-added wood products and services. Photo used with permission of Terry Mace, Division of Forestry, Wisconsin Department of Natural Resources.

LESSONS LEARNED

Product Attributes

Quality wood products The first question asked respondents' opinions on whether a market existed for premium quality hardwoods in the firms' Chinese real estate developments. Observations from previous trade missions revealed that the Chinese market was filled with expensive products at the higher end, but were sometimes low in quality. Not surprisingly, 97 percent indicated that there was such a market. Respondents were then asked what constituted premium hardwood products. Results (Table 12) indicate that attributes related to the environment, durable craftsmanship, and health rose to the top of the list. In many of China's largest cities, the outdoor air quality can sometimes be poor. It was suggested during the interviews that families want the air quality within their homes to be healthy as a place of refuge from the out of doors. Others also have indicated that health is the most important factor to Chinese consumers when choosing interior decorating materials (Butterworth and Lei 2006). It also has been suggested that Chinese consumers are value buyers more than price buyers the cheapest product is not necessarily the most popular product if it is not perceived to be long lasting and high quality (University of Pennsylvania 2006c). Thus, durable craftsmanship was found to be very important to respondents, embedded between the environmental and health attributes.

Good design has been shown in other studies to be important to consumer evaluation of wood products (Brinberg et al. 2007), but was cited only 50 percent of the time by MATi respondents. Perhaps design is an attribute that evolves in importance as other basic attributes, such as product health and durability, improve. It also was interesting that lighter colored woods scored higher than darker colored woods, although generally wood color was not important to perceived quality. Virtually no respondents associated high cost with quality, perhaps indicating the cost conscious nature of the Chinese market. All respondents indicated on a separate question that use of environmentally friendly or energy efficient products was at least somewhat important to their developments (Table 13).

Important attributes for appearance versus functional products
Respondents were asked to indicate the importance of several factors to their sourcing of two different products: staircases and windows. Observations from the trade missions suggested that product types based on appearance (e.g., staircases) might have a different set of attributes associated with them than would more functional or technical product types (e.g., windows). Results show (Table 14) that product quality was clearly the most important factor, followed by healthy finishing (defined as no off gassing) and energy efficiency. Design also was important for staircases, as was availability of professional installation and ease of operation for windows. The desire for professional installation confirmed observations from the trade missions dependable installation services were difficult to find and a potential source of competitive advantage for U.S. producers willing to provide this service with their products.

Table 12.—Percentage of respondents indicating the attributes constituting a premium quality hardwood product

Attribute	Percent
Environmentally friendly	88.2
Durable craftsmanship	81.4
Healthy product	75.5
Long service life	59.8
Good design	50.0
Widely known brand name	46.1
Lighter wood color	44.1
Darker wood color	33.3
High cost	5.9
Other	2.0

Table 13.—Responses to the question, "How important is using environmentally friendly or energy efficient products in your design or development?"

Category	Percent of respondents
Very important	42.2
Somewhat important	57.8
Not important	0.0

While the factors were generally similar for both product types, differences were observed in terms of species used and manufacturing country of origin. In both instances, these were deemed more important for staircases, suggesting an image or status aspect associated with the appearance based wood products.

Species use Given the relative importance of species to appearance based products, respondents were asked to rate the perceived image of a number of U.S. species by Chinese customers for high end architectural wood applications. Walnut and cherry were rated as having the highest status image (Table 15), followed by oak and maple. This seems to contradict the previous finding that darker woods were lower in quality than lighter woods (Table 12), but might reflect the fact that darker woods are more common to Chinese designs and thus lighter woods are associated with imported, higher end products. Rubberwood (*Hevea brasiliensis*), beech (*Fagus* spp.), and ash (*Fraxinus* spp.) fared somewhat poorly in terms of perceived image. Rubberwood is a species common to plantation forest production in Asia and has been increasing in market share in imported furniture pieces to the U.S.

Manufacturing country of origin Numerous studies have shown that country of origin is important to the perceptions associated with certain product categories (Buehlmann et al. 2006). In the current study, while not rated as highly important overall, country of origin was found to be relatively more important to appearance based products (Table 14); this was investigated in more detail and results are shown in Table 16. Nearly half of respondents indicated that premium hardwood products made in China were perceived to be lower in status than those made in the United States. Roughly a quarter each of the remaining respondents indicated that Chinese products were perceived to be higher status or that there was no difference between the two sources, respectively. This would seem to offer a potential competitive advantage to U.S. firms, especially given the positive image of several U.S. species (Table 15). Still, only a minority of respondents indicated a status advantage for U.S. products suggesting that other important factors such as health, craftsmanship, and installation are critical to success for U.S. firms seeking to export to the higher end Chinese market.

Table 14.—Mean responses[a] to the question of how important each factor was to sourcing of wood staircases and wood windows

Factor	Staircases mean	Windows mean
Product quality	4.6 (0.7)[b]	4.5 (0.7)
Healthy finishes (no off-gassing)	4.1 (0.9)	4.2 (0.8)
Energy efficiency	---[c]	4.1 (0.9)
Architectural design	4.0 (1.0)	---
Availability of professional installation	3.9 (0.9)	4.0 (1.0)
Ease of operation	---	4.0 (1.1)
Species used	3.9 (1.0)	3.5 (0.9)
Wood appearance	3.7 (0.9)	3.9 (0.9)
Strong brand name	3.5 (1.1)	3.4 (1.2)
Manufacturing country of origin	3.2 (1.1)	2.9 (0.8)

[a] Scale anchored by 1 not important and 5 very important.
[b] Numbers in parentheses are standard deviations.
[c] Factors not relevant to the specific product.

Table 15.—Mean ratings[a] of perceived species images by Chinese customers for high-end architectural wood applications

Species	Mean	Species	Mean
Walnut	3.9 (1.0)[b]	Cherry	3.8 (1.0)
Oak	3.6 (0.8)	Maple	3.5 (0.8)
Alder	3.3 (0.9)	Rubberwood	3.1 (0.9)
Beech	2.9 (1.0)	Ash	2.4 (1.0)

[a] Scale anchored by 1 low status image and 5 high status image.
[b] Numbers in parentheses are standard deviations.

Table 16.—Percentage of respondents indicating that Chinese products were higher, lower and equal in status to those made in the United States

Category	Percent of respondents
Higher in status than those made in the U.S.	28.9
Lower in status than those made in the U.S.	45.4
Equal in status with those made in the U.S.	25.8

Price sensitivity Lastly, respondents were questioned about the price sensitivity of several sectors of the interior hardwood finishing market in China. Flooring was clearly viewed as the most price sensitive (Table 17), while doors and staircases were viewed as less price sensitive. For U.S. firms seeking to export to China, greater opportunity likely lies with these less price sensitive products, although there was not a large degree of separation between any of the products other than flooring.

Service Attributes

Installation and service after sale An opportunity for competitive advantage observed from the trade missions centered on the provision of installation services. There is essentially no do it yourself market in China. To date, most new construction is simply an unfinished concrete shell which requires substantial finishing (new flooring, staircases, doors, cabinets) prior to occupancy. Often times the installers are not dependable and other than those associated with known entities, such as the big box retailers, there is little accountability for the work done. Interviews on the trade mission with executives from B&Q, a major big box retailer serving mid level markets with 60 stores located in larger cities throughout eastern China, indicated a "pyramid of knowledge" involving manufacturers, retail stores, and installers. Each is a critical link in the Chinese home construction/improvement supply chain.

Installation becomes even more important when considering that reliability (dimensions, opening sizes, etc.) in many residential construction jobs is poor, even in the same development thus it was indicated in the interviews that every construction project in China is a "custom" job given current building practices. In other words, good field measurement is critical. The existence of building codes is very limited in China and those that are enforced are primarily for commercial construction. One further point: there is a trend away from the unfinished shell model and toward sale of new finished condos, which shifts responsibility (and markets) toward developers or their contracted interior finishing companies to make purchasing decisions (Cao et al. 2006). Thus interior decorating in China residential developments may move from a consumer market to an industrial market. There currently are few university graduates in the field of interior design in China (American Hardwood Export Council 2005), which might result in increased demands for decorating and installation services in these markets. Further, to help fill this void, the influence of overseas designers is increasing in China with subsequent demand for higher end U.S. hardwoods (American Hardwood Export Council 2005).

Respondents were asked about installation services (Tables 18 and 19). A majority (89 percent) indicated that trained professional installers are a necessity, and more importantly to potential suppliers, 75 percent of respondents said that provision of professional installation services would help them make more sales. An overwhelming majority (92 percent) indicated that after sale service was very important to them and their customers, compared to the 8 percent who indicated it was somewhat important (no respondent replied that it was unimportant). However, the percentage drops (64 percent) when asked how important it is for the manufacturer to have an office in China for building material products (Table 20). This seems to provide further evidence for opportunity for U.S. exporters who can provide service through contracted representatives or other means.

Table 17.—Mean responses[a] of the price sensitivity of several interior hardwood products in the Chinese market

Product	Mean
Flooring	3.9 (1.1)[b]
Windows	3.5 (1.2)
Architectural mouldings	3.5 (1.3)
Kitchen cabinets	3.4 (0.9)
Staircases	3.2 (1.0)
Doors	3.2 (1.0)

[a] Scale anchored by 1 not price-sensitive and 5 very price-sensitive.
[b] Numbers in parentheses are standard deviations.

Product demonstration   Another opportunity for potential competitive advantage that emerged from the trade missions was related to product demonstration. A majority (68 percent) indicated product demonstration would be useful (Table 21). Clearly, the most frequently cited use for a demonstration showroom was to facilitate communication with customers (Table 22). This was followed by being a sign of status to customers and demonstrating product quality and functionality. Order placement was somewhat infrequently cited.

Product demonstration is part of the bigger challenge of distributing products for display and sale in some parts of China. Estimates suggest that only about 25 percent of the 500 million consumers living in or near the 3,000 largest cities in China are reached by modern retailers. Most other distribution falls to local networks; by the time goods reach the countryside they could be delivered by small cars, motorcycles, or bicycles, and with limited selection available.

Using the example of a durable good such as televisions, 65 to 70 percent of televisions are sold through traditional channels (University of Pennsylvania 2006b). Firms seeking to sell outside of Shanghai, Beijing, or the other largest cities in China must take this into account. However, the larger markets are where the bulk of the current opportunities for value added wood products are located.

Expected delivery times   Expected delivery time was a final consideration from the MATi survey. For solid wood interior doors, custom built exterior doors and windows, and hardwood flooring, a majority indicated that expected delivery time would be 14 days or less (Table 23). However, for custom built kitchen cabinets and custom built stairways, most respondents expected 15 days or more. These latter products likely have the greatest opportunity for U.S. exporters; flooring would seem to be an especially difficult export product for U.S. firms, due to the expectation of quick delivery and price sensitivity (Table 17).

Table 18.—Responses to the question, "In your opinion, are trained professional installers a necessary service for you and your customers?"

Category	Percent of respondents
Yes	89.2
No	0.0
Sometimes	10.8

Table 19.—Responses to the question, "If you could provide professional installation services for wood products, would it help you make more sales?"

Category	Percent of respondents
Yes	78.4
No	0.0
Not sure	21.6

Table 20.—Responses to the question, "How important is it for the manufacturer to have a China office for building material products?"

Category	Percent of respondents
Very important	63.7
Somewhat important	33.3
Not important	2.9

Table 21.—Responses to the question, "In your opinion, would a product demonstration showroom be a valuable tool for you and your customers?"

Category	Percent of respondents
Yes	67.6
No	1.0
Sometimes	31.4

Table 22.—Percentage of respondents indicating the ways a product demonstration showroom would be useful

Category	Percent
It would facilitate communication with customers	83.3
It would be a status sign to customers	63.7
It would be useful to demonstrate product functionality	53.9
It would be useful to demonstrate product quality	53.9
It would be a convenient location for customers to place orders	37.3
Other	3.9

Table 23.—Responses to the question, "When you purchase products, what is the delivery time you expect?"

Product	Within 7 days	Within 14 days	15 to 30 days	Within 60 days
Solid wood interior doors	21.6%	48.5%	27.8%	2.1%
Custom built exterior doors and windows	18.6%	41.2%	33.3%	7.2%
Hardwood flooring	23.7%	34.0%	41.2%	1.0%
Custom built kitchen cabinets	10.3%	24.7%	63.9%	1.0%
Custom built stairways	5.2%	23.7%	60.8%	10.3%

SECONDARY PRODUCERS CASE EXAMPLES

Case 1: Hardwood Flooring Exports to China

An upper Midwestern hardwood strip flooring company has had mixed success in seeking business in China. They do not have an agent representing them in China, but do have an international sales representative which travels to China quarterly. To meet potential clients, they have participated in trade shows in Beijing, Guangzhou, and Dalian with some success. The firm has used the 2008 Summer Olympics to its advantage. Since hard maple is the species of choice for sports floors, the company was able to overcome shipping disadvantages by providing the flooring systems for several Olympic venues in Beijing with this species.

One disadvantage for U.S. flooring manufacturers is the preference for specified lengths within the Chinese marketplace. Most of the hardwood flooring sold in China is 1.0 or 1.5 m long as opposed to the random length solid strip flooring sold in the United States. To capture more markets, domestic producers need to adapt their products to meet the Chinese fixed width and length specifications. In conversations with the buying agents at one Chinese home center during the last trade mission, it was stated that they had carried U.S. produced random length flooring in the past. This product was accepted by the Chinese market; however, the U.S. manufacturer could not produce the volumes necessary to satisfy the demand from the Chinese home center. The home center buying agent stated that they would consider buying U.S. produced hardwood solid strip random length flooring again if they could be supplied in sufficient volumes, but that quantity was beyond the production capacity of this single firm.

Trends in residential flooring in China continue to favor dark colors, especially those of certain tropical species. This flooring company continues to pursue markets within China and may have success in specialty flooring applications, such as sports floors. In addition, the firm is considering hiring an agent to act as a sole representative of their company to help target the higher margin specialty flooring market.

Case 2: Interior Hardwood Stair System Exports to China

Opportunities for value added hardwoods in the Chinese market are the result of increased domestic wealth and the increase in high rise condominium construction. The Chinese condominium buyer purchases an empty concrete shell in contrast to the fully finished units sold in the United States. It is left to the buyer to make provisions for finishing the interior, including electrical, plumbing, wall and floor coverings, cabinets, and more. One such value added product identified by the Chinese home centers during trade mission interviews was hardwood stair systems. Many of the condominium units are multi level. Decorative hardwood stair systems can add value and aesthetics in place of a standard poured concrete stair system.

Examples of high-quality veneered interior doors produced in China. Photo used with permission of Scott Bowe, University of Wisconsin-Madison.

STUDY 2: OPPORTUNITIES AND CHALLENGES FOR SECONDARY PRODUCERS

One Chinese home center stated that hardwood stair systems have been on backorder for months given the limited number of suppliers, and the limited number of qualified installers. A Midwestern stair company is currently looking into an expansion of its stair business into the Chinese marketplace. Options they are considering include production of modular systems in the United States to export to China, or establishment of a production facility in China.

Hardwood stair systems are only one opportunity. The home center industry is booming in metropolitan areas of China. According to Paul Swenson, Director of the Council of Great Lakes Governors trade office, the Chinese home center market currently has money in search of quality wood products, especially at the villa and single family home level. Swenson suggested that some of the following products could be successful:

- Trim, mantels, wainscoting, chair rails, and kicks
- Decorative wall panels
- Kitchen, bath, and utility cabinets
- Interior passage doors
- Closet doors   louvered and solid wood
- Main entry doors
- Wood flooring
- Windows   sunrooms, greenhouses
- Treated lumber kits such as deck kits and wooden playground kits
- Garden products   retaining walls, rails, and fencing

Export of products such as these could serve the growing domestic market within China.

CONCLUSIONS

Secondary Products

Several opportunities for U.S. exports of hardwood products were identified through trade mission observations and the MATi survey. The U.S. currently has a status advantage in high end Chinese markets and seems well positioned to offer key product attributes, including environmentally friendly and healthy products, and durable craftsmanship. Several U.S. species, particularly walnut and cherry, enjoy high status in Chinese high end markets. The United States could be especially well positioned for export of appearance based products with low price sensitivity and longer expected delivery times, such as staircases and cabinets. Interviews during the trade missions suggested that stairway production in particular is a very immature sector in China with strong demand and substantial opportunities for market entry. A key aspect of success seems to be product promotion to Chinese buyers; the survey results support the role that product showrooms can play in communicating to potential Chinese customers. Provision of dependable after sale service, particularly installation services, could enhance the position of U.S. exporters. But even in these higher value markets, price is an important attribute, although Chinese consumers are willing to pay more for perceived value.

RELEVANT BARRIERS TO TRADE

BUSINESS CULTURE DIFFERENCES

Despite decades of trade between the United States and China, estimates of a combined $6 billion in wood products exports between the two countries in 2007 (Wagner 2007), and the opportunities described in this report, many challenges still exist. Several issues emerged from the trade missions and surveys. Some of the key challenges include business culture differences, different technical terms and standards, access to quick market information, and transportation barriers from the interior United States.

Business Relationships
In the United States, sales can sometimes be initiated by phone calls or emails without meeting face to face because there are reliable policies to guarantee the quality of products and prompt payment. But in China, this arrangement is risky before a solid relationship is established. Trustworthy relationships are not easy to establish unless there is a close connection with the company's high level management. Establishing a sales relationship can best be achieved by direct meetings and conversations. Online sales currently are not reliable in China. Therefore, contacts found online or through company websites are not ideal without an established relationship.

Price Quotes
The use of price quotes is common in China, which has a price driven market. Price lists or quotes are the first things customers will ask for before discussing any product specifications, such as quality or grade. Price quotes are easy to obtain in China, but also easy to change from the time of the quote to the close of the sale. The quote on paper does not hold any force of law in China, which means easy come and easy go. In the United States, a price quote is often viewed as a commitment between the seller and buyer. Therefore, clear communication is critical for initiating relationships and establishing long term commitments between business representatives from the two countries.

TECHNICAL TERMS AND STANDARDS

The complicated U.S. hardwood lumber grading system and other technical standards are difficult for many Chinese customers to understand, especially those who do not speak English. It could take a long time for the Chinese customer to learn the rules and realize the products that they receive may not be what they thought they were paying for. Establishing relationships and trust is critical. It may be effective for both sides to communicate about the buyers' specific needs and then customize products with the price to create win win situations.

ACCESS TO QUICK MARKET INFORMATION

The Chinese market and associated manufacturers are regionalized in business climate, consumption patterns, infrastructure, logistical systems, and government roles. For example, the furniture and flooring manufacturers are concentrated along the coastal areas, such as Guangdong, Fujian, and Zhejiang provinces, mainly to be positioned for the export market. To export American lumber or even value added products to China, brand promotion or advertisement is important. With Chinese manufacturers clustered, market information can spread quickly. Any changes in raw material demands and/or customers preferences can cause dramatic market shifts. Being among the first to discern such changes can provide a big advantage for U.S. hardwood producers.

TRANSPORTATION BARRIERS, ESPECIALLY FROM THE INTERIOR U.S.

When exporting wood materials to China, interior locations, such as the Lake States, can sometimes face a transportation cost disadvantage when compared to states more proximate to coastal ports (Fig. 3). Products with more added value might be able to absorb these added transportation costs if the higher margins are significant. Companies operating in interior areas can overcome freight disadvantages by making value added customized products or entering the export market when there are a high demand for certain products, and then continuing promotion and business relationships to compete for long term export markets. Exporting by state as a percent of total production is analyzed below

Table 24.—State GDP in wood products (NAICS 321), wood products exports, and wood products exports as a percent of GDP for states in the eastern hardwood forest region

State	GDP in wood products, 2005 (million $)[a]	Exports of wood products, 2006 (million $)[b]	Exports as % of GDP
New York	625	238	38.1
Vermont	178	46	25.8
Connecticut	102	23	22.5
Maine	510	97	19.0
Kentucky	708	127	17.9
Ohio	1,209	214	17.7
Pennsylvania	1,933	334	17.3
Michigan	892	148	16.6
New Hampshire	227	37	16.3
Missouri	485	79	16.3
North Carolina	1,933	302	15.6
New Jersey	339	52	15.3
Florida	1,531	229	15.0
Virginia	1,402	208	14.8
Indiana	1,299	191	14.7
West Virginia	628	86	13.7
Maryland	278	38	13.7
Tennessee	1,071	137	12.8
17 other states	---	---	below median
Median (n 35)	708	86	12.8

[a] U.S. Department of Commerce, Bureau of Economic Analysis (n.d.)
[b] U.S. Department of Commerce, International Trade Administration (n.d.)

for two major NAICS categories for wood products. The 35 states included comprise the eastern hardwood forest region, as defined by the Wood Education and Resource Center (www.na.fs.fed.us/werc/).

Wood Products Manufacturing

For wood product manufacturing (NAICS 321), which includes lumber, plywood, veneer, wood containers, wood flooring, wood trusses, manufactured homes, and prefabricated wood buildings, international exports as a percent of total production ranged from 38.1 to 1.8 percent across the 35 states investigated. The median export rate was 12.8 percent (Table 24). It seems that states both proximate and distant to port locations scored above the median.[6] Some of the states notably distant, and with relatively large GDP in wood products, included Indiana, Tennessee, Michigan, Kentucky, and West Virginia.

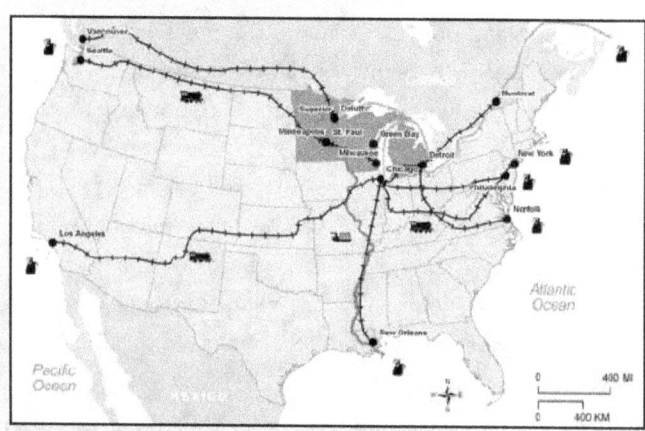

Figure 3.—Major shipping routes within the United States, relative to the Lake States region.

[6] The States' 2006 per capita trade budgets (using data from the State International Development Organizations [SIDO] for state trade division budgets and Census population data for 2000) also seemed to have little to do with the state rankings those states above the median export rate for wood products budgeted a median of $0.34 per resident on trade and while states in the lower half of exporting rates budgeted a median of $0.35 per resident. This measure must be interpreted with caution since it represents data for a single year and state expenditures for trade programs can change from year to year. Other factors also come into play, including the behavior of individual firms within given states and the export value of the existing resource base in terms of species and/or quality.

Furniture and Related Product Manufacturing

Data also were available for furniture and related product manufacturing (NAICS 337), which includes furniture, mattresses, window blinds, cabinets, and fixtures. Here, international exports as a percent of total production ranged from 20.6 percent to 1.1 percent across the 35 states investigated. The median export rate for furniture and related products was 7.5 percent (Table 25). Again, it seems that states both proximate and distant to port locations scored above the median. Some of the states notably distant, and with relatively large GDP in furniture and related products, included Michigan, Wisconsin, Illinois, Tennessee, and Minnesota.

Discussion of Transportation Barriers

An issue that emerged from this project was that for states closer to the interior of the eastern United States, it might be more feasible to export secondary or value added products rather than primary products due to shipping costs. For some states with relatively large output of both primary products (defined here as NAICS 321, wood products manufacturing) and secondary products (defined here as NAICS 337, furniture and related products), this seemed to be the case. Notably, Wisconsin (with $1,551 million in primary products GDP) and Minnesota (with $1,306 million in primary products GDP) ranked above the median for exports of secondary products (Table 25) but below the median for exports of primary wood products.

In sum, there seems to be wide variety among states in terms of exporting forest products with no clear patterns emerging based on location, although distance to ports does sometimes appear to play a role. A final point is that across the 35 states included in the analysis, the median exporting rate is higher for primary products than for secondary products, suggesting that U.S. firms, at present, generally are geared more toward exporting raw materials and not finished products.

Table 25.—State GDP in furniture and fixtures (NAICS 337), furniture and fixture exports, and furniture and fixture exports as a percent of GDP for states in the eastern hardwood forest region

State	GDP in furniture and fixtures, 2005 (million $)[a]	Exports of furniture and fixtures, 2006 (million $)[b]	Exports as % of GDP
Louisiana	102	21	20.6
Florida	1,110	176	15.9
Connecticut	218	34	15.6
Maryland	236	30	12.7
New York	1,110	134	12.1
New Jersey	582	66	11.3
Illinois	1,119	126	11.3
Ohio	1,738	187	10.8
Texas	1,704	181	10.6
Tennessee	914	94	10.3
Michigan	3,798	388	10.2
Wisconsin	1,260	126	10.0
South Carolina	174	17	9.8
Maine	65	6	9.2
Kentucky	361	30	8.3
Mississippi	1,427	109	7.6
Minnesota	853	64	7.5
North Carolina	3,060	228	7.5
17 other states	---	---	below median
Median (n 35)	840	34	7.5

[a] U.S. Department of Commerce, Bureau of Economic Analysis (n.d.)
[b] U.S. Department of Commerce, International Trade Administration (n.d.)

Many states offer export assistance for resident companies that are interested in exploring export opportunities. The following directory provides a starting point for producers interested in exploring international trade opportunities within the eastern hardwood forest region. It does not necessarily represent all of the trade assistance resources available in a given state. All websites were current as of October 21, 2008.

- **Alabama** Development Office, Office of International Trade ✧ www.ado.alabama.gov/content/ourservices/international trade/trade main.aspx
- **Arkansas** Economic Development Commission ✧ www.arkansasedc.com/business development/international business.aspx
- **Connecticut** Department of Economic & Community Development ✧ www.ct.gov/ecd/site/default.asp
- **Delaware** Office of Management and Budget ✧ http://itc.omb.delaware.gov
- Enterprise **Florida**, Exporting Assistance ✧ www.eflorida.com/ContentSubpage.aspx?id=466
- **Georgia** Department of Economic Development ✧ www.georgia.org/Business/International
- **Illinois** Department of Commerce and Economic Opportunity, Office of Trade and Investment ✧ www.commerce.state.il.us/dceo/Bureaus/Trade
- **Indiana** Economic Development Corporation, Office of International Development ✧ www.in.gov/iedc/international.htm
- **Iowa** Department of Economic Development, International Office ✧ www.iowalifechanging.com/business/export assistance.html
- **Kansas** Department of Commerce, Trade Development Division ✧ www.kansascommerce.com/IndexPages/Div04a.aspx
- **Kentucky** Cabinet for Economic Development, International Trade Division ✧ www.thinkkentucky.com/kyedc/internationaltrade.aspx
- **Louisiana** Economic Development Department ✧ www.lded.state.la.us
- **Maine** International Trade Center ✧ www.mitc.com
- **Maryland** Department of Business and Economic Development, International Operations ✧ www.choosemaryland.org
- **Massachusetts** Office of International Trade and Investment ✧ www.moiti.state.ma.us
- **Michigan** Economic Development Corporation ✧ www.michiganadvantage.org/Expand Your Business/Export Assistance/Default.aspx
- **Minnesota** Department of Employment and Economic Development, Minnesota Trade Office ✧ www.exportminnesota.com
- **Mississippi** Development Authority, Trade Bureau ✧ www.mississippi.org/content.aspx?url=/page/3280&

- **Missouri** Department of Economic Development, Business and Community Services ✧ www.missouridevelopment.org/Business%20Solutions/Global%20Business%20Assistance.aspx
- **Nebraska** Department of Economic Development, Office of International Trade and Investment ✧ www.neded.org/content/view/78/137/
- **New Hampshire** Division of Economic Development, Office of International Commerce ✧ www.nheconomy.com/international trade/
- **New Jersey** Office of Economic Growth ✧ www.nj.gov/njbusiness/international/
- **(New York)** Empire State Development ✧ www.nylovesbiz.com/Small and Growing Businesses/global markets.asp
- **North Carolina** Department of Commerce ✧ www.nccommerce.com/en/BusinessServices/InternationalBusiness/
- **Ohio** Department of Development, Global Markets Division ✧ www.odod.state.oh.us/itd/ServicesForExporters.htm
- **Oklahoma** Department of Commerce ✧ www.okcommerce.gov
- **Pennsylvania** Department of Community and Economic Development ✧ www.NewPA.com/trade
- **Rhode Island** Economic Development Corporation ✧ www.riedc.com/business services/international trade and exporting
- **South Carolina** Department of Commerce ✧ www.sccommerce.com/businessservices/export development.aspx
- **Tennessee** Department of Economic and Community Development ✧ www.state.tn.us/ecd/bizdev idg.htm
- **Texas** Office of the Governor, Economic Development and Tourism ✧ www.governor.state.tx.us/ecodev/
- **Vermont** Department of Economic Development, Agency of Commerce and Community Development, Vermont Global Trade Partnership ✧ www.economicdevelopment.vermont.gov/Programs/GlobalTrade/tabid/121/Default.aspx
- **Virginia** Economic Development Partnership, Division of International Trade ✧ www.exportvirginia.org
- **West Virginia** Development Office, International Division ✧ www.wvdo.org/international/index.html
- **Wisconsin** Department of Commerce ✧ www.commerce.state.wi.us/IE/

American Hardwood Export Council. 2005. **China market report: July/August 2005**. Washington, DC: American Hardwood Export Council. 9 p.

Barford, M.A. 2004. **Mark my words. In: The Standard: a newsletter for the Appalachian Hardwood Manufacturers, Inc.** [High Point, NC]: Appalachian Hardwood Manufacturers, Inc. September: 6.

Boardman, P. 2006. **China's building boom.** Presentation at China's Boom: Implications for Investment and Trade in Forest Products and Forestry. 2006 January 18 20; Vancouver, BC. Madison, WI: Forest Products Society. www.forestprod.org/internationaltrade06 powerpoints.html.

Bowe, S.; Bumgardner, M.; Wang, X. 2007. **An assessment of hardwood lumber markets in China.** In: Buckley, David S.; Clatterbuck, Wayne K., eds. Proceedings, 15th central hardwood forest conference; 2006 February 27 March 1; Knoxville, TN. e Gen. Tech. Rep. SRS 101. U.S. Department of Agriculture, Forest Service, Southern Research Station: 460 469. [CD ROM].

Braden, R. 2006. **Opportunities and constraints for wood building materials: The challenge of China.** Presentation at China's Boom: Implications for Investment and Trade in Forest Products and Forestry. 2006 January 18 20; Vancouver, BC. Madison, WI: Forest Products Society. www.forestprod.org/ internationaltrade06powerpoints.html.

Brinberg, D.; Bumgardner, M.; Daniloski, K. 2007. **Understanding perception of wood household furniture: application of a policy capturing approach.** Forest Products Journal. 57(7/8): 21 26.

Buehlmann, U.; Bumgardner, M.; Lihra, T.; Frye, M. 2006. **Attitudes of U.S. retailers toward China, Canada, and the United States as manufacturing sources for furniture: an assessment of competitive priorities.** Journal of Global Marketing. 20(1): 61 73.

Bumgardner, M.; Hansen, B. 2001. **Hardwood market trends: lumber exports to Asia.** Tech. Paper 01 P 17. Rockville, MD: Forest Resources Association Inc. 5 p.

Butterworth, J.; Lei, Z. 2005. **China, Peoples Republic of, solid wood products annual 2005.** GAIN Report Number CH5052. Washington, DC: United States Department of Agriculture, Foreign Agricultural Service. 27 p.

Butterworth, J. and Lei, Z. 2006. **China, Peoples Republic of, solid wood products annual 2006.** GAIN Report Number CH6052. Washington, DC: United States Department of Agriculture, Foreign Agricultural Service. 16 p.

Cao, X.; Hansen, E.N.; Xu, M.; Xu, B. 2004. **China's furniture industry today.** Forest Products Journal. 54(11): 14 23.

Cao, J.; Braden, R.; Eastin, I. 2006. **Distribution systems for value-added wood products in China.** CINTRAFOR Working Paper 102. Seattle, WA: University of Washington. 68 p.

Global Wood Trade Network. 2006. **Industry news & markets: China wood products prices.** Global Wood. September 16 30, 2006. www.globalwood.org/ market1/aaw20060902d.htm. [Date accessed unknown].

Global Wood Trade Network. 2007. **Industry news & markets: China wood products prices.** Global Wood. June 1 15, 2007. www.globalwood.org/market1/ aaw20070601d.htm. [Date accessed unknown].

Hardwood Market Report. 2005. **2004: The year at a glance.** Memphis, TN: Hardwood Market Report. 130 p.

Hardwood Review. 2007. **Starved for optimism? A hardwood export boom may be just around the corner.** Hardwood Review. 24(6): 1, 21, 23.

International Tropical Timber Organization. 2006a. **Report from China. In: Tropical Timber Market Report.** [Yokohama, Japan]: International Tropical Timber Organization. 11(5): 11 12. www.itto.or.jp/. [Date accessed unknown].

International Tropical Timber Organization. 2006b. **ITTO's annual review 2005: exports**. In: Tropical Timber Market Report. [Yokohama, Japan]: International Tropical Timber Organization. 11(12): 10 13. www.itto.or.jp/. [Date accessed unknown].

International Tropical Timber Organization. 2007. **Report from China**. In: Tropical Timber Market Report. [Yokohama, Japan]: International Tropical Timber Organization. 12(9): 9 10. www.itto.or.jp/. [Date accessed unknown].

Jiang, Z. 2007. **Current situation and future development: the forest products industry in China**. Forest Products Journal. 57(7/8): 6 15.

National Hardwood Lumber Association. 2003. **Rules for the measurement & inspection of hardwood & cypress plus NHLA sales code & inspection regulations**. Memphis, TN: National Hardwood Lumber Association. 136 p.

Petry, M.; Qing, Z. 2007. **China, Peoples Republic of, solid wood products, Chinese wood usage continues rapid growth**. GAIN Report Number CH7057. Washington, DC: U.S. Department of Agriculture, Foreign Agricultural Service. 20 p.

Schuler, A.; Buehlmann, U. 2003. **Identifying future competitive business strategies for the U.S. furniture industry: benchmarking and paradigm shifts**. Gen. Tech. Rep. NE 304. Newtown Square, PA: U.S. Department of Agriculture, Forest Service, Northeastern Research Station. 15 p.

U.S. Census Bureau. n.d.a. **New privately owned housing units started** [Database]. www.census.gov/const/www/newresconstindex.html. [Date accessed unknown].

U.S. Census Bureau. n.d.b. **Median and average square feet of floor area in new one-family houses completed by location, and median and average square feet of floor area in units in new multifamily buildings completed** [Database]. www.census.gov/const/www/charindex.html. [Date accessed unknown].

U.S. Department of Commerce, Bureau of Economic Analysis. n.d. **Regional economic accounts – gross domestic product by state** [Database]. www.bea.gov/regional/gsp/. (18 January 2008).

U.S. Department of Commerce, International Trade Administration. n.d. **Tradestats express home** [Database]. http://tse.export.gov/. (18 January 2008).

University of Pennsylvania. 2006a. **One billion, three hundred million: the new Chinese consumer**. Knowledge@Wharton. October 16, 2006. http://knowledge.wharton.upenn.edu/article/1572.cfm. (11 September 2007).

University of Pennsylvania. 2006b. **Navigating the labyrinth: sales and distribution in today's China**. Knowledge@Wharton. October 16, 2006. http://knowledge.wharton.upenn.edu/article/1573.cfm. (11 September 2007).

University of Pennsylvania. 2006c. **Selling to the local Chinese market: an interview with Lenovo's Deepak Advani and BCG's Hal Sirkin**. Knowledge@Wharton. October 16, 2006. http://knowledge.wharton.upenn.edu/article/1575.cfm. (11 September 2007).

Wagner, O. 2007. **China, Peoples Republic of, solid wood products, China's wood processing sector and re-exports of imported U.S. wood materials**. GAIN Report Number CH7061. Washington, DC: United States Department of Agriculture, Foreign Agricultural Service. 17 p.

White, A.; Sun, X.; Canby, K.; Xu, J.; Barr, C.; Katsigris, E.; Bull, G.; Cossalter, C.; Nilsson, S. 2006. **China and the global market for forest products: transforming trade to benefit forests and livelihoods**. [Place of publication unknown]: Forest Trends. 31 p.

Zhu, G. 2006. **General situation of Chinese wood market and export**. Beijing: China Timber Distribution Association. [Number of pages unknown].

www.ingramcontent.com/pod-product-compliance
Lightning Source LLC
Chambersburg PA
CBHW080754290526

45790CB00008B/3438